PESTS

How to control them on fruit and vegetables

Pauline Pears and Bob Sherman

garden organic

GARDEN ORGANIC/SEARCH PRESS

The authors would like to thank Lawrence D. Hills, founder and President of the HDRA and a guiding light to many an organic gardener.

Published in Great Britain 2006

Search Press Ltd
Wellwood, North Farm Road,
Tunbridge Wells, Kent TN2 3DR

in association with

Garden Organic
Ryton Organic Gardens
Coventry CV8 3LG

Originally published in 1990 as *Pests: how to control them on fruit and vegetables* and in 1992 as *Pests: how to control them on fruit and vegetables – revised edition*

Illustrations by Polly Pinder
Photographs by Charlotte de la Bédoyère
All the photographs in this book have been taken in organic gardens, and all of the fruit, vegetables and flowers pictured have been grown organically.

The Publishers would like to thank the following for allowing them to photograph their animals: The Burstow Wildlife Sanctuary for the hedgehog and the jay which appear on pages 3 and 21 respectively; Mrs H.A.C.T. Clark for the bat which appears on page 12; Mrs Nicky Edwards of The Wise Owl Pet Shop for the rabbit which appears on page 24.

The Publishers would also like to thank Andrew Halstead for his help in the preparation of this book.

ISBN 1 84448 156 5

Printed in Malaysia by Times Offset (M) Sdn, Bhd

Conversion Chart

From centimetres to inches		*From grammes to ounces*	
1 cm	= ½ in	7g	= ¼ oz
2.5 cm	= 1 in	14g	= ½ oz
5 cm	= 2 in	28g	= 1 oz
10 cm	= 4 in	110g	= 4 oz
50 cm	= 20 in	450g	= 16 oz (1lb)
100 cm (1m)	= 40 in	*from litres to pints*	
1sq m	= 1.2 sq yds	1l	= 1.75 pt

Exact conversions from imperial to metric measures are not possible, so the metric measures have been rounded up.

Note referring to the scale of the pictures
The actual size as shown with some of the pictures is approximate only, as some of the creatures do in fact vary in size quite considerably.

Introduction

The obvious way of dealing with pests organically is to swap a chemical spray for one that is called 'organic'. But, although the 'organic' sprays may be safer than some, they are certainly not harmless and should never be seen as the mainstay of any pest control strategy. There is a whole range of effective alternatives, techniques and tricks that can be used to keep pests in check which do not rely on the use of sprays.

There are, for example, ways of making your garden more attractive to the beneficial creatures that are natural pest controllers. Also, organic methods of soil care result in vigorous, well-balanced plants which will be less attractive to pests and diseases; so this enables the plants to resist attack.

When and how to sow and plant are important factors in ensuring that plants grow without any problems. Pest build-up can be minimized by crop rotation and good hygiene, and pests kept at bay by the use of barriers and traps.

Success with any form of pest control is improved if the problem is first correctly identified. Although it is difficult to cause much harm by using the wrong method of organic control, a lot of time and effort can be wasted in trying to control the wrong pest! The charts on pages 40-43 will help you with the identification process.

The organic gardener should never aim to wipe out every pest (what a Herculean task that would be!), but just aim only to reduce pests to an acceptable level. Learning more about the pests in your garden, either by reading and/ or observation, will help to prevent panic. You will soon learn how much damage plants can tolerate without being harmed. The presence of a pest does not necessarily mean that it is going to be a problem.

The best way to achieve an acceptable level of pest control is to use a combination of several of the techniques covered in this book. The pesticides that are permissable for use in an organic garden are described at the end of the book, but their use should be kept to a minimum, as they can harm creatures other than the pests at which they are aimed.

Also, whenever a spray has to be used, the gardener should be looking for ways to avoid the problem arising in future seasons.

The much loved hedgehog should be encouraged to stay in your garden to feast on slugs.

Know and encourage your friends

Take a stroll around your garden and you'll soon notice all sorts of tiny creatures going about their business. The more you look, the more you will see ....

At this stage it is all too easy to assume that these creatures are hell–bent on eating your favourite plants. Most of us have been brought up to regard anything that creeps, crawls, wriggles or squirms as something 'nasty'. In fact most of the creatures in your garden are harmless and even useful. They are working hard to prevent pests and diseases from getting out of hand.

Every pest and disease has its own predatory pest and disease. If this were not so, we would be crawling with caterpillars and knee deep in greenfly. The aim in an organic garden is to help these 'beneficial' creatures in their work and to try and tip the balance in their favour. The first step is to stop using chemical sprays that can harm them. In the past, creatures have actually been turned into pests as a result of sprays killing off their natural enemies. The fruit tree red spider mite *Panonychus ulmi,* for example, was not a pest until the 1920's, when tar oil winter washes and other sprays were introduced. Until then, mite numbers had been kept down by a host of natural enemies including lacewings, capsids, beetles and predatory mites. The winter washes killed these natural enemies, but allowed the red spider mite to breed unchecked, reaching levels which made it a serious pest. Other insecticides only compounded the problem. This is a well-documented example of pesticides actually creating pest problems, but there are surely many more which have not yet been studied.

The second step in helping our garden friends is to get to know them (so they are not killed in error) and to keep them happy by supplying them with suitable sources of food and shelter.

We cannot always rely on these natural creatures to keep pests down to the levels we would like, but they play a significant part and we would be lost without them. This chapter introduces some of our 'garden friends' – from mites, insects, and beetles to frogs, lizards and birds, and suggests ways we can encourage them to live and work in our gardens.

Identifying garden friends

The ladybird is one of the best known of our garden friends. Both adults and developing larvae do a useful job in eating greenfly and other aphids, scale insects, mealy-bugs, thrips and mites. Adult ladybirds hibernate in winter and have to start eating soon after they wake in spring. A clump of nettles can provide a useful early breakfast, as nettle aphids, which do not trouble other plants, are one of the earliest to appear.

Actual size x 14

Actual size x 9

Ladybirds

The red and black adult ladybird below (Coccinella 7-punctata) is much too pretty for anyone to take for a pest, but the slaty-blue crawling larvae above are not always so lucky, and can cause alarm when they appear in numbers on garden plants. Top right is a ladybird pupa (a stage between larva and adult).

There are many kinds of ladybirds including red ones with only two spots, black ones with red spots and, as illustrated on page 4, yellow ones with black spots (Propylea 14-punctata).

Actual size x 11

Hover-fly Syrphus ribesii

Actual size x 9

Parasitic wasps

Actual size x 10

The larvae of the parasitic wasp Cotesias glomerata emerging from a large white caterpillar.

6

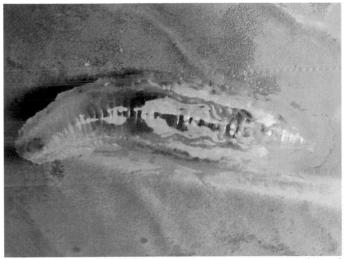

Actual size x 7

Actual size x 3

Hover-fly

On page 6 is Syrphus ribesii, one of the many hover-fly species. Hover-flies have flatter bodies and tend to be smaller than wasps. They all hover silently and do not sting! The adults feed on pollen and nectar while the larvae (above) are the ones that eat aphids and other small pests. The larvae can also be green.

Another attractive 'friendly' insect is the hover-fly. Unfortunately it is often mistaken for a wasp (*see page 26*), but once you get to know them the difference is easily spotted. Hover-fly larvae are not difficult to find; you only have to look amongst a colony of aphids. Just one larva can eat one aphid per minute!

The more adult hover-flies eat, the more eggs they lay, so it is worth providing them with a good supply of food. They will take nectar and pollen from a whole range of flat, open, single flowers, such as *Limnanthes douglasii* (the poached egg plant), *Convolvulus tricolor*, fennel, buckwheat and many others, (*see page 13*).

There is also an abundance of parasitic wasps and flies in the garden that kill a whole range of pests including aphids, caterpillars, scale insects, root fly larvae and whitefly. Parasitic wasps Aphidius are tiny and rarely noticed, but the damage they do to pests can easily be seen.

Another common sight, later in the season, is a large white cabbage caterpillar, surrounded by yellow, almost fluffy looking cocoons. These are the young of another parasitic wasp, *Cotesias glomerata*, which have been living and feeding within the caterpillar.

Aphid shells

If you look at a colony of aphids, you may see some straw-coloured 'shells' with a small hole, as above. This is a sure sign that tiny parasitic wasps (Aphidius), shown below, have been at work. They lay their eggs inside the aphids where the young live, then grow until they are ready to cut their way out, leaving hapless, dead aphids in their wake. The picture above shows both live and dead aphids.

Actual size x 6

Lacewing
There are several types of lacewings, so-called because of their beautiful 'gauze-like' wings which are green or fawn. The ones pictured here are Chrysopa septempunctata.

Earwig
Many people shudder at the sight of earwigs (Forficulidae). They are often automatically 'squashed' as a pest despite the fact that they eat codling moth eggs and woolly aphids. Earwigs can be mild pests but their good points outweigh their bad.

Actual size x 5

Actual size x 6

All these tiny wasps and flies are attracted to the flat flowers of the Umbellifer family, such as carrots, parsnips and fennel. They also like the *Compositae* (daisy-type) flowers which include Michaelmas daisies, mustard and yarrow. The Compositae also provide nectar and pollen for the delicate lacewing, whose voracious larvae feed on aphids and other soft-bodied creatures. The adults enjoy a few insects too, but they need a supply of pollen, especially when laying eggs.

Earwigs and ground and rove beetles, the large black scuttly ones, are also useful. Ground and rove beetles are shy creatures who appreciate a garden with lots of cover, such as thick leaf or bark mulches, ground cover plants etc. They will be rare in a garden where the soil is bare, every last scrap of vegetation cleared away, and the grass scalped to a bowling–green.

Rove beetles

There are many different rove beetles (Staphylinidae), mostly black and brown in various sizes. All are shy and fast moving and can be seen easily at night. They enjoy slugs, root aphids, root fly larvae, other pests and their eggs.

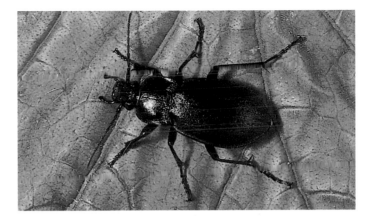

Ground beetles

There are large numbers of ground beetles (Carabidae). They vary in size from 5 to 25 mm, and they are predators of many garden pests, including slugs.

Anthocorid bug

There are many varieties of anthocorid bugs. The one below is Anthocoris nemorum, one of the smallest. There are brown and black ones, and they are important predators of fruit and vegetable pests: aphids, root aphids, capsid bugs, caterpillars, midges, blossom weevils and red spider mite.

Centipedes, not to be confused with millipedes, also appreciate a mulch to hide in while they rest between meals of slugs and other pests. A little bit of studied 'untidiness' will make a garden much more attractive to many useful creatures.

Centipedes

These creatures are 'friends' unlike the millipede in the bottom picture, which is a nuisance, (see also page 24). There are various varieties of centipedes which have only one pair of legs per segment, whilst millipedes have two.

Actual size x 4

Actual size x 4

Actual size x 4

10

Frogs and toads
Frogs (top right) eat slugs, and toads (below right)
account for large numbers of insects, that is if you are
lucky enough to have them in your garden.

Garden ponds are becoming popular in these conservation conscious days, which can only be a good thing. They may be responsible for the current frog population, which remains relatively healthy despite the fact that there has been a vast reduction in the number of ponds in the countryside. Lucky is the gardener who can attract slug-eating frogs to live and breed in the pond.

Hedgehogs seem to be much more popular than frogs, having a 'cuddly' image despite the fact that they are unpleasant to hug! They are welcome in the garden as yet another slug-eater. Encourage one to stay by providing a hibernating site like a pile of logs or autumn leaves under a hedge, or even a custom-built hedgehog box.

Someone else who appreciates somewhere to hide is the slow-worm. These snake-like creatures are in fact legless lizards and are totally harmless to humans – but not to slugs!

Slow-worm
These creatures are often mistaken for snakes and are
now not a common sight. They should be encouraged,
as slugs form a principle part of their diet. They can
grow up to 50 cm long.

Although some birds can be a nuisance in the garden, many are extremely valuable and should be encouraged. Nesting boxes and fat on a string when food is scarce may encourage blue tits to make their home with you. These busy birds are experts at winkling out codling moth cocoons in winter and aphid eggs from the gnarled bits of apple tree bark. They can account for ninety-five per cent of codling moth cocoons. When digging a plot where pests are overwintering, robins and other birds are always welcome. Their eagle eyes soon spot a tasty morsel, which they are quick to seize upon.

It may be difficult to regard spiders with affection, but they should be seen as welcome guests. Many species living in orchards and gardens are useful predators, and they are always more abundant on unsprayed sites. Different species of spider will vary in their diet, but this can include spider mites, aphids, codling moths, winter moths and their larvae, leafhoppers, midges and other small insect pests.

Bats
These creatures, hunted almost to extinction in the past due to their association with horror vampire stories, are now a protected species in many parts of the world. Bats will eat up to 3,500 insects in one night, so it is worth encouraging them to stay.

Glow-worm *(Lampyris noctiluca)*   *Actual size x 8*
The glow-worm is a creature associated with old pastures and woodland edges. Changes in land use, with consequent loss of habitat, mean that they are now fairly rare. The picture shows the male larva, which does not glow as brightly as the female, but both live on slugs and snails.

The beneficial creatures introduced here are just a few of many that can be found in nature. Make your garden a friendly place for wildlife and it will repay you handsomely. Not only will pests and diseases diminish, but the garden will be a nicer place to be.

So, next time a creepy–crawly scuttles across your path, don't squash it – it could be a friend.

Plants for attracting and feeding wildlife

The lists on this page show some of the many plants that can attract and feed wildlife, including our garden friends. Some have flowers that provide food in the form of nectar and pollen. Others, such as wild cherry and hawthorn, will provide a supply of 'pests' to keep the beneficials going when none are available elsewhere in the garden.

The annuals are easy to grow in and around the vegetable plot, as well as in flower beds.

The wild flowers and perennials could be introduced into a herb bed, ornamental border or 'wild area' as appropriate. It is not perhaps usual to grow flowers amongst fruit trees and bushes, but a bed with, say, a spring planting of ordinary carrot and parsnip roots could be very beneficial, as well as attractive. Many gardens are too small to accommodate trees and large shrubs, but there might well be room for a few grown as a hedge.

Whatever the size of your garden, there should be room in it for at least a few 'attractant' plants which will help keep pest levels down and look attractive too.

A - annual HA - hardy annual HHA - half-hardy annual B - biennial P - perennial

TREES AND SHRUBS

Wild cherry *Prunus avium*		April
Bird cherry *Prunus padus*		May
Wild crab apple *Malus sylvestris*		May
Rowan *Sorbus aucuparia*		May
Hawthorn *Crataegus monogyna*		May
Buckthorn *Rhamnus cathartica*		May/June
Blackthorn *Prunus spinosa*		March/April
False acacia *Robinia pseudoacacia*		June
Mock orange *Philadelphus coronarius*		June/July
Willow *Salix* spp.		March onwards
Guelder rose *Viburnum opulus*		May/June
Spindle *Euonymus europaea*		May/June
Spiraea *Spiraca* spp.		May-July

WILDFLOWERS AND 'WEEDS'

Meadow clary *Salvia pratensis*	P	June-July
Dandelion *Taraxacum officinale*	P	April-June
Clover *Trifolium* spp.	P	May-Oct
Cow parsley *Anthriscus sylvestris*	P	April-June
Nettles *Urtica* spp.	P	May-Sept
Wild strawberry *Fragaria vesca*	P	April-July
Hawksbeard *Crepis biennis*	B	May-July
Sea holly *Eryngium maritimum*	P	July/Aug
Yarrow *Achillea millefolium*	P	June-Nov

Sainfoin *Onobrychis viciifolia*	P	May-Sept

Cultivated relatives of this list should also act as zattractants, unless they are highly bred 'double' forms.

CULTIVATED ANNUALS

Poached egg plant *Limnanthes douglasii*	HA
Cornflower *Centaurea cyanus*	HA
Viper's bugloss *Echium vulgare*	HA
Californian poppy *Eschscholzia* spp.	HA
Buckwheat *Fagopyrum esculentum*	HHA
Annual convolvulus *Convolvulus tricolor*	HHA

The flowering period of these plants will vary with sowing time. Hardy annuals can be sown in the autumn to produce flowers early in the following spring.

The wild relatives of these cultivated species may also be grown as attractant plants.

CULTIVATED PERENNIALS

Angelica *Angelica archangelica*	July/Aug
Fennel *Foeniculum vulgare*	July-Sept
Michaelmas daisy *Aster* spp.	Aug-Nov
Shasta daisy *Chrysanthemum maximum*	July-Sept
Golden rod *Solidago* spp.	July-Sept
Pearl everlasting *Anaphalis* spp.	August
Globe thistle *Echinops* spp.	July/Aug

VEGETABLES

Carrot *Daucus carota*	B	June-Aug
Parsnip *Pastinaca sativa*	B	June-Aug

Avoid problems

Get the soil right

The previous chapter concentrates on ways to improve the environment above ground. It is equally important to look at the environment below ground – i.e. the soil, which is where a large part of most plants grow.

The aim is to create soil conditions which encourage unchecked, balanced plant growth. Plants grown in such conditions will be less attractive to pests and diseases, and more able to resist attack.

The physical conditions

It is unreasonable to expect a plant to grow healthily in a soil that is waterlogged, hard as a rock, or bone dry. A good soil is the basis of effective organic growing, so it is essential to take some time and trouble either to improve the physical conditions of a poor soil, or maintain the quality of a good soil.

Organic manures and composts will help considerably, finally resulting in a soil that is crumbly enough for roots to grow through without difficulty, yet still able to hold sufficient water. Our first handbook *How to make your Garden Fertile* gives a detailed guide to making and using compost, and other organic materials that will help to create a good soil. Good management techniques are also important, such as not working soil that is too wet or too dry, and avoiding excessive digging.

Even organic materials cannot solve severe drainage problems however, which should be sorted out beforehand. This information can be found in good general gardening books.

A good diet

Chemical fertilizers dissolve quickly in the soil which means that a plant can over-feed. Where too much nitrogen is available, the result may be lush, sappy growth, which is just what pests and diseases like. The food contained in organic fertilizers and manures, on the other hand, is only slowly available to the plant, as the materials must first be broken down by the living organisms in the soil. The resulting plants are sturdier and 'harder' and less attractive to pests.

If you are starting a garden from scratch, it is worth having the soil tested to find out whether the pH (acid/alkaline balance) is reasonable for what you want to grow, and that the soil is not lacking in any particular mineral. If necessary, shortfalls can be made up using rock minerals and other organic fertilizers. This is particularly important when planting fruit trees and bushes, which will be in the same site for a long time. It is difficult to correct a deficiency once the ground has been planted up.

Shifting the balance

Just as pests and diseases above ground have their enemies, so do those living in the soil. These are often on a microscopic scale. Anything you do to improve the soil for growing plants will also encourage these natural pest controllers. They appreciate a soil rich in organic matter, and one where harmful soil insecticides are not used.

A good start

Seedlings and young plants are very vulnerable, especially when weather and soil conditions mean that growth is slow. To avoid disaster at this stage, do everything possible to encourage quick emergence and growth.

For example: wait till the soil warms up, or warm it with cloches before sowing. Later sowings will often overtake earlier ones anyway. If the soil tends to set hard, cover seed drills with compost, leaf mould or even a peat/sand mix. This will allow seedlings to come through quickly. Germinating seeds before sowing (pregermination) can also speed up seedling growth.

Raising seedlings indoors allows you to start before the soil has warmed. They should be well hardened off before planting out.

Buying in plants

Some very nasty pests (such as potato eelworm) can unwittingly be brought into a garden in the soil around the roots of seedlings and plants. Many pests are too small to be seen with the naked eye, so the only way to be sure that this does not happen is to obtain all plants and seedlings from a reputable source, or to raise everything yourself. The latter option is fine for vegetables (apart from potatoes), but propagating fruit plants from your own stock is not advisable unless you are certain that they are one hundred per cent healthy.

The right site

Plants will only grow strongly if they are planted in a situation they enjoy; in the right sort of soil, with the right amount of sunlight (or shade) and protection from the wind. Unhappy plants are always more prone to problems. Gardens do not always provide ideal sites but do the best you can and check before you plant.

Resistant varieties

If you have a persistent problem the answer may be to grow 'resistant' varieties. Examples of these are given under the appropriate crops, but check the catalogues too, as new ones are being introduced all the time. If a variety is resistant to a pest, it does not mean that it is *immune*. However, the effects will be less.

Breaking the cycle

If crops such as brassicas or onions are growing all year round, pests can reach epidemic proportions because a suitable host plant is always available. Break the cycle by clearing up all the plants of one type before more of the same are sown. This can help to solve the problem.

The same principle applies to fruit when planting new stocks. Always remove and destroy any old plants that are suffering from a persistent pest or disease *before* introducing the new.

Winter digging

Some pests pass the winter in the soil. Their numbers can be reduced by turning the ground over in winter to expose them to the cold and to predators such as birds.

Also, netting should be removed from the top of the fruit cage over winter to allow the birds in to do their work.

Companion planting/ intercropping

The idea of growing one plant next to another to keep pests at bay is very attractive. Several books have been written listing 'good companions'. Unfortunately there is little evidence that these actually work. However companion planting carrots and onions is effective as it keeps carrot fly at bay (*see page 32*). Brassicas and beans planted together keep aphids and root fly from the brassicas (*see page 31*). Research trials show that details such as plant numbers, timing, etc., must be right for the 'companionship' effect to work.

Know your problem
Before tackling a problem, it is important to know whether you are dealing with a pest, a disease, a virus, a deficiency in the soil or even some environmental factor. Only then can you decide whether anything needs to be done and if so, what. It is very frustrating and a waste of time and energy trying to deal with the wrong cause.

It is helpful to know the life cycle and habits of a pest in order to devise ways of avoiding or coping with it.

Crop rotation

Crop rotation simply means that the same type of plant is not grown on the same piece of ground every, year. Rotation prevents drastic build up of soil-living pests and diseases and makes soil management simpler.

In the vegetable garden, for example, moving the potatoes to a different plot each year will help to reduce the buildup of eelworm – if you are unlucky enough to have this pest. By doing this the eelworms will have nothing to feed on until potatoes are planted in this same plot several years later.

Also, because the potato crop is the one that tends to be manured, it means that, over a period of years, the whole vegetable garden is treated. A three or four year rotation is good, but a five or six year cycle (if this is possible) is even better.

An example of a four year rotation is given here, but there are many variations on this theme. Gardeners usually work out the rotation that suits themselves and their vegetables best.

When planning a rotation there are two factors to bear in mind:

1. Keep together the crops that are prone to the same pests and diseases (see box below).
2. Keep together the plants that like the same soil conditions.

Plant groups that are prone to the same pests and diseases:

● Potatoes and tomatoes
● Onions, garlic, leeks, shallots
● Cabbages, Brussels sprouts, cauliflower, kale, sprouting broccoli, calabrese, swede, turnip, kohlrabi, radish, mustard
● Carrots, parsley, parsnips, celery
● Peas and beans of all sorts; winter tares
● Courgettes and pumpkins

In the fruit garden, annual rotation is not practical. The plants would not appreciate the moves! But new stock should always be planted on a new site, as far away as possible from the old one.

An example of a four year rotation

Year 1: potatoes.

Year 2: legumes (peas, beans, etc).

Year 3: brassicas (the cabbage family).

Year 4: root crops, including onions, but excluding any brassica root crops.

YEAR I
POTATOES
ROOTS
BRASSICAS
LEGUMES
YEAR 2
LEGUMES
POTATOES
ROOTS
BRASSICAS
YEAR 3
BRASSICAS
LEGUMES
POTATOES
ROOTS
YEAR 4
ROOTS
BRASSICAS
LEGUMES
POTATOES

Other crops, such as lettuces, courgettes etc., are fitted in where appropriate, but should still be moved round in rotation.

Protecting your plants

Netting

Flying pests from pigeons and blackbirds to flea beetles and greenfly can be kept at bay with netting. Just choose the mesh size of the net to suit the pest.

Ordinary plastic garden netting is most useful for keeping out cats, dogs, birds, and other large pests. A smaller mesh netting with mesh of 1 cm square or less can be used to protect brassicas from the cabbage white butterflies.

Very small pests such as flea beetles and root flies can be kept out using the fine mesh nets or lightweight spun polyester materials that are now available. Some are used over a framework, (cloche hoops are ideal), but others are so light and soft that they can be laid directly on top of the plants. These porous materials have the advantage over plastic covers in that they let air and water through, so only need to be removed for weeding.

Important: Cover plants *before* the pests arrive. Plants can either remain covered throughout their life, or just while they are particularly vulnerable.

Plastic garden netting.

Fine mesh nets or spun polyester materials make excellent protective coverings for plants.

Commercial 'humming line' to keep off birds (see page 21).

Fencing

A good fence is really the only effective method of keeping rabbits out of a garden. It should be made of a material with a mesh size of 5 cm or less. To prevent the creatures burrowing underneath, wire netting should be buried in the ground as illustrated.

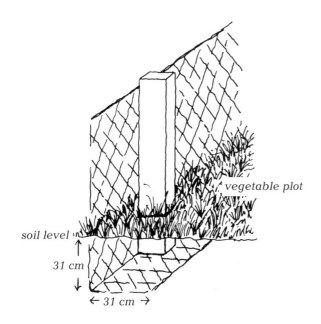

Electric fencing against rabbits is now also possible. It is movable, and avoids the hard work of erecting a conventional fence, but the initial expense will be greater.

Root fly barriers

Plants of the cabbage family can be protected from the cabbage root fly by placing a 13 cm square of rubbery carpet underlay on the soil

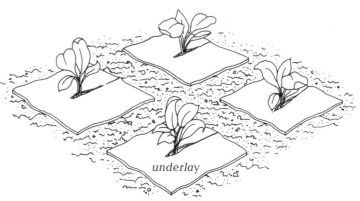

around the stem at planting time. A barrier of a different type can be used to exclude the carrot root fly.

A sturdy barrier, 75 cm high, made of polythene or very fine netting, will keep carrot root fly at bay. A size of around 90 cm by 3 m works well. Put it up before, or immediately after sowing.

18

Bottle cloches

Individual cloches can be made by cutting off the bottom of a plastic drinks bottle. These cloches afford protection against many pests including slugs - as long as you don't trap one inside! They also keep off cold winds and create a warmer atmosphere for the plants.

Traps

A variety of home-made and commercially available traps can be used to reduce pest numbers. They are unlikely to achieve a long-term reduction, but may help protect crops in the short-term.

Leaf weevils, which can congregate in hordes on raspberries, are easily caught on greased boards held under the canes while the foliage is shaken. Use a heavy grease (like car grease) or one of the non-drying sticky glues that are readily available. Similar boards can be used to catch flea beetles, which jump up when plants are disturbed.

Codling moths can be caught in a sticky trap, to which they are lured by a synthetic 'sex attractant' (pheromone) available from gardening suppliers. The wingless winter moth females can be stopped on their journey up the trunk of a fruit tree by a sticky grease band, (see page 38).

The preparation used for this purpose is a special vegetable grease. Ordinary car grease should not be used.

In the vegetable plot, home-made traps can be used for slugs, wireworms and millipedes.

A synthetic sex hormone lures male codling moths to a sticky end in this trap.

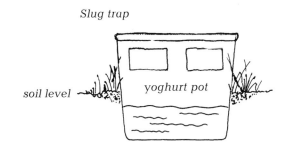

Slug trap

soil level

yoghurt pot

beer or milk and water

Hand picking

Nip problems in the bud by picking off infected shoots and leaves at an early stage. Summer pruning of soft fruit bushes has a similar effect. Larger pests such as caterpillars and slugs are easily removed by hand.

19

General fruit and vegetable pests

This chapter should be used with the identification charts at the back of this book, see pages 40-43.

The pests described here are not particularly fussy in their choice of food and therefore can be a problem to a wide range of totally unrelated plants

---

Aphids
Fruit and vegetables

These small, soft-bodied insects come in a range of colours, but are often lumped together under the same name 'greenfly' or 'blackfly'. Some types of aphid will attack only a single, or a small number of species of plant. Others have wider tastes. The one pictured above on this page is the potato aphid, the one below is a lettuce leaf aphid.

Aphids tend to live in fast-growing colonies. They feed on plant sap and this activity weakens and distorts growth. They secrete a sticky 'honeydew', which falls on to leaves and pods on which black sooty moulds grow. Sooty moulds are not in themselves harmful, but they prevent light getting to the leaves, cause premature leaf fall, and spoil the appearance. Some species protect themselves by making leaves pucker and curl, or by living under a woolly coating which makes control difficult. Aphids can also transmit viral diseases.

Aphids overwinter both as eggs and sometimes as adults. In the spring winged youngsters fly off to infest lush, young plants. They breed quickly, producing live, wingless offspring. When the plants begin to mature, winged aphids are again produced and these fly off to new host plants. Some will remain there for the winter, while others will fly off to overwinter on a plant unrelated to the summer host.

Prevention
Plants with correct growing conditions and a balanced food supply are much less attractive to aphids.

Their natural enemies are legion: including hover-flies, ladybirds, parasitic wasps, anthocorids, spiders, earwigs and birds. The section 'Know and encourage your friends' beginning on page 4 describes ways to encourage these creatures in the garden. Remember that many of these beneficial creatures need aphids to feed and breed on, so where aphids are not causing any real problem, leave them as reserve food supplies, to keep your 'friends' happy.

Once infested
Infested leaves, shoots etc., can be picked off, or the aphids knocked off with a strong jet of water.

Note: some more specific methods of dealing with aphids are listed in the 'Crop by crop' section.

Actual size x 13

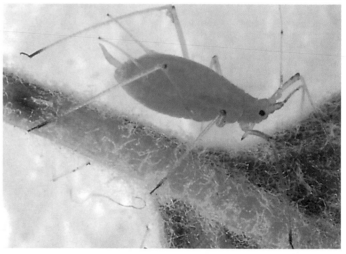

Actual size x 14

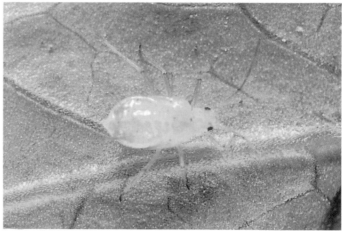

Birds
Fruit and vegetables

Birds account for enormous numbers of pests, but unfortunately they themselves can also be pests. Fruit, in particular, is a great favourite of several common birds, especially the jay pictured above, and bullfinch damage to winter buds of fruit bushes and trees can be severe. Pigeons are a problem for vegetables, destroying a cabbage patch in no time at all.

Prevention
Marauding birds soon get used to most scaring devices, so to be at all effective these devices should be changed every week or so.

Winter bullfinch damage may be reduced by providing alternative food sources, e.g. seed heads of teasel etc., which the finches prefer.

Netting susceptible crops is the only really effective method of preventing attack. Where the risk is less, scaring techniques, can be tried, such as:
● Video, computer or cassette tape, stretched between canes. This will flash in the light and make a noise in the wind.
● Commercial 'humming line', which also makes a noise in the wind (*see page 18*).
● Pieces of hosepipe laid out to look like snakes.
● Children's plastic windmills and anything else that flaps, turns or makes a noise in the wind.

Capsid bugs
Mainly fruit

There are a number of species of this small shield-shaped winged bug, some specific to certain host plants such as the potato capsid and apple capsid, but the common green capsid has widespread tastes. All bush or tree fruits are potential food sources for capsids. They feed on leaves, buds and flowers leaving irregular ragged holes in leaves whilst flowers, buds and fruits are distorted. Apples show raised bumps and irregularities in shape but are perfectly edible and can be stored.

Capsids feed at night, move fast and are very hard to catch. Fortunately plants can usually

Actual size x 6

tolerate their damage, so long as virus is not transmitted through injection of saliva, in which case there is no effective method of control.

Cats and dogs

Remember your much loved pets can create havoc in the garden. Cats can be excluded from seed drills or sensitive seedlings with low netting or pea sticks. It is advisable to train your dog not to go on the garden.

Cutworms   Vegetables

Cutworms are large, squashy, soil-living caterpillars. They vary in colour but all curl up like a 'C' when disturbed. They feed at night on the soil surface, eating off young plants at ground level. They often work along a row, leaving wilting and dead specimens in their wake. Cutworms also feed on stems, roots and tubers of crops such as celery, beetroot, carrots, potatoes and strawberries.

22

These pests are the caterpillars of various moth species, which lay their eggs on plants, and plant debris in June/July. The caterpillars feed for a couple of months before they are ready to become moths. These moths again lay eggs and the resulting caterpillars overwinter in the soil, feeding whenever the weather is warm enough. They pupate in the spring.

Actual size x 4

Prevention
Where cutworms have been a problem, winter digging may reduce their numbers. Blackbirds love them. The most efficient answer, if you have them, is to let a flock of hens run over the plot – when it is fallow of course!

Individual plants can be protected with collars of tin or plastic drainpipe, pressed down a few centimetres into the soil.

Once infested
During the growing season, individuals may be picked up by hand, from just under the soil surface in daytime, or on it at night. Regular hoeing helps to disturb them.

Earwigs   Fruit
Forficula auricularia

These brown insects, with prominent pincers at one end, have a worse reputation than they deserve (*see picture on page 8*). They are powerful predators and eat a considerable number of insect eggs, including those of the codling moth. They are only a minor pest of fruit trees, although they do damage some fruit, especially apples. They are often found hiding round apple stalks, but generally only use cavities on fruits, or other damage already created by birds and wasps, for concealment rather than feeding. Damage to flowers and leaves is likely to be slight.

Damaged apples have small, slightly discoloured soft patches, punctured by tiny black feeding holes. Such fruit is edible but will not store.

Since earwigs are more of a friend than an enemy, try not to kill them. This is a diffcult task anyway.

Leather-jackets
Vegetables

Tipula spp. and Nephrotoma

This soil-living pest is the larva of the familiar gangly 'daddy-long-legs' or crane-fly.The larvae are a dull, greybrown colour and are mainly a pest of lawns in autumn, spring and summer. They also feed, however, on the roots of some vegetable crops; brassicas in particular. Normally they are only a problem on soils recently prepared from old lawns or pastures or on particularly weedy plots. Sometimes they may persist for a few years after initial cultivation, but damage should decrease gradually.

Actual size x 4

There are no suitable sprays or soil treatments for this pest. Regular cultivation and the maintenance of a weedfree plot should reduce damage.

Mice and Voles
Vegetables and fruit

Field mice can cause havoc in early spring and autumn sowings of peas and beans. Voles are very partial to beetroot and carrots and will also nibble Jerusalem artichokes and potatoes, especially those grown on a no-dig system. Voles also cause damage to roots of fruit bushes and trees.

Prevention

Conventional traps can be set outdoors, preferably under some form of cover so that other animals and birds are not caught. An alternative is to use 'humane' traps, which catch mice alive.

If mice are a real problem, keeping a cat may be a good deterrent.

If seeds of peas and beans are being eaten, it may help to delay sowing until early summer when more food is around for the mice. Well-grown transplants are less likely to be eaten. Beans can be raised in home-made paper pots; rows of peas in lengths of plastic guttering. These can be suspended above the ground if mice attack them too!

If mice and voles are seriously damaging tree roots, it is advisable to apply no surface mulch.

Millipedes
Vegetables

Millipedes are slim, many legged, segmented creatures, up to 6 cm long. They move quite slowly and smoothly, coiling up like a spring when at rest. They have two pairs of legs per segment (unlike the fast moving centipedes which have one pair per segment, (see page 10) and can be one of several colours including shiny black, yellow with red spots, and brown and white.

Actual size x 2

Millipedes feed mainly on dead plant material such as leaf litter and wood, but they will also eat young seedlings. They will extend wounds in tubers and roots made by other creatures but are not able to initiate this sort of damage. You will always find the damage below ground level but it is not easily recognizable as being caused by millipedes. The only way to be sure is to look in the surrounding soil for the pest.

Millipedes live and breed in the soil, especially in undisturbed accumulations of plant debris. They prefer moist soil, rich in organic matter. They are not an easy pest to control.

Prevention
On a small scale, millipedes may be distracted from seedlings with a millipede trap. A trap can be made with a piece of cut potato or carrot skewered on a stick, or stuffed into perforated tin cans and buried in the soil. These should be replaced regularly and any trapped millipedes disposed of.

Digging the soil will disturb them and expose them to attack by their enemies which include birds, hedgehogs, frogs, toads and ground beetles.

Rabbits

Rabbits can consume a whole crop in one night if present in numbers, (*see the chapter on 'Protecting your plants; on page 17*).

Slugs and snails   Fruit and vegetables

Four species of slug are common garden pests. They range in colour from pinky/fawn to black and reach up to 10 cm in length. They feed on a wide range of plants. Seedlings may be eaten off as they come up, larger plants reduced to shreds, and fruit, roots and tubers eaten to hollow shells. Often a tell tale slime trail identifies the culprit.

Slugs lose water rapidly in dry weather and they dislike light, so feeding tends to be by night and on dull days after rain. Damage is always worse in warm wet weather.

In autumn, some species will move down into the soil as the temperature drops; others can keep feeding at very low temperatures 1–2°C (33–35°F).

Slug eggs are transparent or opaque little globules, found in cavities in the soil and are laid at almost any time of year.

Coping with slugs

There is no simple, single method of coping with slugs organically. The ideas included in the following list have all worked for someone at some time; a combination of several is more likely to succeed.

● Encourage quick seedling germination and growth. *(see page 14)*

● Transplant from modules or pots rather than bare root; harden off well.

● Cover plants with plastic bottle cloches (but don't trap a slug inside),

● Surround plants with a wide barrier of dry materials such as sawdust, bark, woodash or soot. Rain will soon reduce their effectiveness, but cloches may help.

● Lay out old lettuce leaves between young seedlings as an alternative food supply. Slugs prefer dead and dying plants and will be attracted to them to feed. The slugs can then be picked off at night. If the leaves are covered with something to keep them moist, such as a roof tile, or piece of wood, they will last longer, and the slugs feeding on them can be picked up during the day.

● Handpicking and trapping are unlikely to have any long-term effect on slug numbers but can give protection at vulnerable stages. Pick slugs off plants at night (by torchlight). Many will collect under wet cardboard or newspaper and can then be collected and dropped into salty water, or squashed etc.

● Traps, consisting of a yoghurt pot half buried in the soil and filled with beer or milk, may catch large numbers *(see page 19)*. Alter the bait now and again, and stop using traps if they catch ground beetles as they eat slugs.

● Where potato slugs are a problem, harvest the crop by early September as this is the month in which most damage is caused.

● An autumn-dug soil, left rough, helps slugs survive a bad winter by allowing them to go far down into the soil to hibernate. If you must dig, do it in the cold of winter for maximum distruption of eggs and slugs.

● If you keep a flock of hens on the land, or some ducks, they will make short work of the slugs. If you can't keep such livestock, try to encourage other slug enemies – hedgehogs, frogs, toads, ground beetles, and slow-worms.

● As a last resort see page 46.

Swift moth caterpillars
Hepialus spp.

Fruit and
vegetables

Swift moth caterpillars are white with a shiny brown head and they can be up to 6.5 cm in length. They live in the soil and feed on roots and tubers. They also eat into the stems of plants.

The moths lay eggs from June to August, in weedy ground for preference. The caterpillars are a common sight when ground is being cleared. They feed through the winter and may continue for another year before maturing into adults.

Actual size x 4

Prevention
Regular weed control will limit egg laying, and winter digging may reduce numbers in the soil. If weedy land being brought into cultivation is seen to contain this pest, it should be thoroughly cleared and cultivated before planting up.

Wasps
Paravespula spp.

Fruit

Wasps are so familiar that they need no description. Fertile queens build small papery nests in the spring to start a nuclear brood which, when hatched, continue to expand the nest rapidly, building large colonies under suitable conditions. Surprisingly much of their diet consists of caterpillars, aphids and insects and it is only in high summer and autumn that they become a major pest of all fruit, sometimes stripping a plum to leave nothing but a dry stone hanging from the tree. In dry hot summers damage will be worse because of increased numbers.

Prevention
Jam jars part filled with sugary water, or jam and water, and suspended in trees will catch many wasps. Derris dust can be used, see page 46.

Weevils, leaf
Fruit and vegetables

Ceutorhynchus spp., Phyllobius spp.

Weevils are a type of beetle, easily distinguished by their pointed snouts. They feed on leaves of a number of different plant groups, including peas, beans, brassicas and some fruit. Leaf weevils of fruit (Phyllobius spp.) have a metallic bronze or green sheen and feed on leaves of raspberries, pears and other tree fruits in May and June. Damage is seldom severe but an infestation can temporarily check plant growth.

Actual size x 13

Prevention and once infested
A greased board held under a branch where weevils are feeding will catch hundreds at a time if the branch is shaken.

Wireworms
Strawberries and vegetables

Agriotes spp.

Wireworms are slender, yellowy-brown, beetle larvae with tough shiny skins; they have three pairs of legs at the head end of the body. They can grow up to 2.5 cm in length.

Wireworm feed on the underground parts (stems, tubers, roots) of many vegetables, including lettuce, onions, tomatoes, potatoes, beetroot, carrots, peas, beans and strawberries. The amount of damage depends on the stage of growth and vigour of the plants. Seedlings wilt and die; older plants may survive, possibly with reduced vigour. Lettuce and tomatoes are at risk at a later stage because the wireworm tunnels up into the stem. Mature potato tubers and carrot roots are also attacked, the initial small hole often being enlarged by other pests.

Wireworm are the larvae of the click beetle which lay its eggs in summer, mainly in grassland or weedy soil. The resulting larvae feed for up to five years, the main feeding period being from March to May. They also feed, less actively, in September and October.

Because they do not like being disturbed, wireworm can often be found in large numbers in pasture and rough land.

Actual size x 2

Prevention
If old grass or pasture land is being brought into cultivation, the best time is February and March. Wireworms will be feeding in the turf, and if this is buried deeply the wireworm should stay down with it, feeding for a couple of years before coming up to cause damage. If land is kept weed-free, the wireworms should have flown after five years, with no new ones to replace them.

Sometimes wireworms remain a problem even on cultivated land. Various strategies can be used to help reduce the damage:

● Encourage quick germination and growth of seedlings, (see page 14).

● Sow into a firm seedbed and delay thinning as long as possible.

● Cultivate the land, to expose them to the birds that eat them.

● In small areas wireworm can be caught in pieces of potato or carrot spiked on sticks and buried in the ground. These should be replaced regularly.

● Peas and beans are less attractive to wireworm than other crops.

● Harvest potatoes by early September, to limit autumn feeding damage.

Vegetable pests, crop by crop

This chapter should be used with the identification charts at the back of this book, see pages 40-43.

Asparagus

Asparagus beetle *Crioceris asparagi*
These distinctive chequered beetles and their plump grey/black larvae are the main pest of asparagus, feeding on the foliage and stems from May onwards. Persistent attacks may check growth.

Actual size x 7

Prevention
● In the autumn, clear up accumulated plant debris from the bed, as this is where many beetles will spend the winter.

Once infested
● As a last resort, see page 46.

Beans   Broad, French, runner

Bean seed fly *Delia platura*
Small white maggots feed on germinating pea and bean seeds early in the season. Seedlings die or fail to appear. Worst in cold springs when growth is slow.

Bean seed flies emerge from the soil in late spring and lay their eggs in soil or on seedlings.

Prevention
● Encourage quick early growth, *(see page 14),* or use transplants.

● Fork the soil over two weeks before sowing.
● Sow under a protective cover, (see page 17).

Once infested
● There is no cure.

Actual size x 9

Bean weevil (*see Picture above and 'Pea and bean weevil', page 34.***)**

Blackfly Black bean aphid *Aphis fabae*
Black 'greenfly' form colonies on the growing tips; they may then spread to the rest of the plant,

including pods. A severe infestation can stunt growth and reduce the crop.

Blackfly overwinter as eggs on spindle bushes and appear first on the tips of broad beans in May. As the plants mature the blackfly move on to other beans (French and runner), beetroot, leaf beet and chard, and ornamentals such as nasturtiums, poppies and dahlias. The blackfly that infest elder trees are a different species.

Prevention
● Sow broad beans in the autumn, so that the plants are tougher and less attractive in the spring.

Once infested
● Pick out infested tips of broad beans.
For more information see 'aphids' on page 20

Blossom or pollen beetle *Meligethes aeneus*
Small, shiny black beetles appear in large numbers around June/July, having just left the flowering oilseed rape crops. The beetles can be found on and in a wide range of flowers, including runner beans. They are often blamed for poor runner bean crops but, although they do eat pollen, they do not prevent pod set and no control measures are necessary. Poor cropping is generally a result of hot, dry soil and air conditions.

One crop that pollen beetles can harm is calabrese; they graze the calabrese heads, making them unattractive to eat.

Prevention
● Calabrese crops can be protected by covering the plants with a fine, lightweight material *(see page 17)*, before the pests arrive.

Once infested
● There are no good measures to take once the beetles have infested a plant.

Beetroot and spinach beet

Black bean aphid *(see 'Blackfly' page 28.)*

Leaf miner *Pegomya hyoscyami*
Leaves show blotchy brown 'blisters', made by the leaf miner grub. This can check growth on young plants; it is not really a problem on older beetroot, but it looks unpleasant on leaf beet and tends to be worse in cool weather.

Eggs are laid under leaves in spring; the larvae eat into the leaves to feed for a few weeks then return to the soil to pupate. There are two or three generations a year.

Prevention
● Winter dig where this pest was a problem.
● Encourage quick early growth *(see page 14)*. Grow plants under a protective cover, *(see page 17)*.

Once infested
● Squash larvae within the leaves.
● Pick off infested leaves.

Brassicas
including broccoli, Brussels sprouts, cabbage, Chinese cabbage, calabrese, kale, kohlrabi, radish, swede and turnip.

Mealy cabbage aphid *Brevicoryne brassicae*
This 'floury' grey aphid forms large colonies on leaves which become distorted and discoloured. A severe attack can kill young plants, or prevent them from cropping. Older plants are less troubled.

Mealy aphids are present all the year round, spending the winter as adults or eggs on winter brassicas and move to new young plants in the spring.

Prevention
● Break the cycle: bury all winter brassica stumps, as soon as cropping has finished, in the compost heap or compost trench. Do this *before* any new susceptible plants are put out.

Once infested
● Check plants regularly, especially newly planted seedlings, from June on. Squash the aphids, or see page 20.

Caterpillars, large white *Pieris brassicae*
(Caterpillars illustrated top right, eggs second right, butterfly third right.)
These are impressive yellow and black caterpillars which feed on leaves and they vary in size enormously. The leaves of young plants may be stripped completely, and those of older plants reduced to holes and tatters. Eggs are laid in groups on the undersides of leaves in April/May, July/Aug and in September in some regions. Note the beautiful symmetry of the eggs.

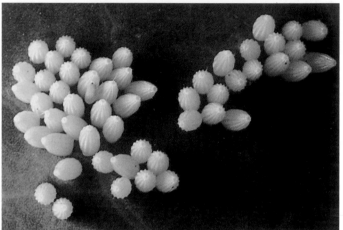

Caterpillars, small white *Pieris rapae*
(Caterpillar illustrated bottom right)
These caterpillars are smaller, solitary, and velvety green. Eggs are laid singly in March/April, June/July and, the peak laying season, August/September. Damage as for large white.

Caterpillars, Cabbage moth *Mamestra brassicae*
(Not illustrated)
These are large plump caterpillars ranging from light green to brown. They feed on leaves and bore into the hearts of cabbages and cauliflowers. There is only one generation a year, with eggs laid in May/June.

Prevention
● Grow under netting with a mesh of 1 cm square or less *(see page 17).*

Once infested
● Squash eggs and pick off caterpillars. As a last resort, see page 46.

Cabbage root fly *Delia radicum*
(Not illustrated)
Stunted and wilting brassica plants are usually the first sign of this pest. The plants are easily pulled

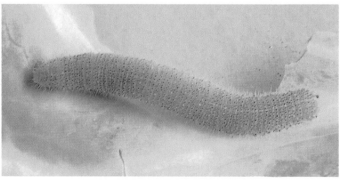

up because the small white root fly larvae have eaten away the roots. Older plants can survive an attack, though in the case of root crops (radish, turnip, swede) they can be rendered inedible.

Root flies overwinter as small brown shiny cocoons in the soil. Adults hatch when cow parsley comes into flower (early May), and lay their eggs in the soil around brassica plants. The second generation (July/August) is the most troublesome in oilseed rape growing areas; there may also be a third.

Prevention
    Winter dig the soil after an infected crop.
    Rotation.
    Break the cycle, (see cabbage whitefly opposite).
    Grow under a protective cover, (see page 17).
    Put 12 cm square mats of rubbery carpet underlay around young transplants.
    Intercrop with beans, (see box below).
    Raise transplants in 7-8 cm, or bigger pots, so that they have a good root system when planted out.

Once infested
    Earth up stems to encourage new root growth.

Intercropping for cabbage pest control
Intercropping plants of the cabbage family with other, unrelated, plants will reduce the damage caused by both cabbage root fly and mealy aphids. It seems that the mixture misleads and confuses the pests, so fewer root fly eggs are laid, and fewer aphids colonize the brassicas. The increased ground cover intercropping gives also encourages natural predators, such as ground beetles.

Research shows that dwarf broad and French beans are both good for intercropping. Grow brassicas and beans in alternate rows 25 cm apart. The outer rows must be beans. For a good crop from both beans and brassicas, the plants need to be about the same size when planted out. If you want a mixture of summer cabbage and French beans, sow the cabbage about three weeks before the beans. Plant out when a reasonable size. French beans should at least have their first pair of leaves fully grown. If they do not, the diversionary tactics of the mixture do not work immediately which is just when the brassica plants are at their most vulnerable.

Brassica whitefly *Aleyrodes proletella*
This is a common pest which usually looks much worse than it is! Tiny white flies live on the undersides of leaves and fly up in a cloud when disturbed. They may make leaves sticky with honeydew, which turns into harmless sooty moulds.

Whitefly can be found on brassicas all year round. They stop breeding in the winter but can still be active.

Actual size x 30

Prevention
● Break the cycle. Remove all overwintered brassicas in the early spring, before new plants are transplanted. Bury all old plants in the compost heap, or in a compost trench.

Once infested
● Pick off lower leaves infested with whitefly larvae. As a last resort see page 46.

Flea beetles *Phyllotreta spp.*
These small dark shiny beetles are a pest of brassicas and other related crucifers, eating small holes in leaves of seedlings and also of larger plants of the more tender brassicas such as Chinese cabbage. Losses can be severe, especially in hot dry seasons.

Actual size x 9

Flea beetles hibernate in plant debris, and under loose bark on trees. They first appear in April or May (when midday temperatures reach 20°C (68°F)). Eggs are laid in the soil and new adults start to feed in August.

Prevention
● Encourage quick early growth, *(see page 14)*.
● Sow/transplant under a protective cover *(see page 17)*.
● Ensure seedlings and young plants are never short of water.

Once infested
● Use a sticky board, *(see page 19)*, to trap the beetles which jump up as plants are disturbed. As a last resort see page 46.

Blossom/pollen beetles
See Bean section on page 29.

Carrots

Carrot root fly *Psila rosae*
Carrot root fly larvae feed on roots of carrot, celery, celeriac, parsnip, parsley and chervil. Seedlings may be killed; older plants may show a reddening of the leaves and growth may be stunted. Roots will have 'rusty' coloured galleries tunnelled in them and small white larvae may be present. If damage is severe carrot roots may be inedible.

Carrot root fly overwinter in the soil, and in roots left in the ground, emerging in May/June to lay eggs in the soil near suitable crops; the larvae feed for a month then pupate in the soil. A second generation of adults will emerge in Aug/Sept.

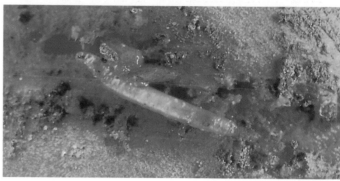

Actual size x 13

Prevention
● Rotation.
● Sow carrots in Feb/ early March or delay till June.
● Grow on a windy site.
● Dig over land that has been infected to let the birds at the pupae.
● Intercrop four rows of onions between each row of carrots. This protective effect lasts only until the onion leaves stop growing. They stop when the bulbs start to form.
● Grow under a protective cover, *(see page 17)*, or within a carrot fly barrier, *(see picture on page 18)*.

Once infested
● Carrots and parsnips for use during the winter should be lifted in the autumn and stored in a shed. Left in the ground, carrot root fly damage will continue and get worse.

Celery

Celery fly/leaf miner *Euleia heracleii*
Larvae tunnel within leaves of celery, celeriac and parsnip, causing blotchy brown 'mines' which later dry up to give a scorched look. A bad attack can stunt growth and make celery tough.

Celery flies emerge from the soil in spring to lay eggs on suitable leaves. The larvae feed for a month then pupate in leaf or soil. There are up to three generations a year, so this pest can be a problem all season.

Prevention
● Grow plants under a protective cover, *(see page 17)*.

Once infested
● Pick off infested leaves, or squash the larvae within them to reduce future generations.

Lettuce

Lettuce root aphid *Pemphigus bursarius*
Infected plants will be stunted and may wilt suddenly. A closer look will reveal white 'floury' aphids on the roots.

This aphid usually spends the winter on poplar trees, moving on to lettuces in June, but some may remain in the soil over winter.

Prevention
● Grow resistant varieties, e.g. Avonchisp, Avondefiance.
● Rotation.
● Winter digging.

Once infested
● Remove infested plants, to reduce spread.

Lettuce leaf aphids *various*
Three sorts of aphids can infect lettuce leaves. A heavy attack can make the crop unpalatable and stunt growth. Check young plants regularly and deal with the problem as shown on page 20.

Onions and related crops
including, spring onions, garlic, leeks, shallots, and chives.

Onion fly *Delia antiqua*
These flies attack onions, shallots and leeks. The fly larvae (white maggots, up to 1 cm in length) feed on roots, killing young plants and damaging bulbs which then rot.

Adults look like small house-flies and emerge from the soil in May, to lay their eggs on, or near, suitable plants. The larvae hatch out and feed for three weeks, then return to the soil to pupate. There may be two or three generations a year, but the first is the worst.

Prevention
● Rotation.
● Winter dig infected land.
● Grow under a protective cover, *(see page 17)*.

Once infested
● Remove infested plants to reduce spread.

Stem eelworm *Ditylenchus dipsaci*
This microscopic pest can attack a wide range of plants - fruit, ornamentals, weeds and vegetables. On onions the leaves swell and distort, bulbs crack and rot. Plants will crop badly, and may die. Similar symptoms occur on leeks and garlic.

Once the plants begin to rot, this eelworm moves back into the soil where it can survive for a considerable time even in the absence of a host.

Prevention
● Rotation.
● Grow only brassicas and/or lettuce (which this eelworm does not attack) on the infested plot for the next two years, and keep it weed-free. It should then be safe to return to onion growing.

Once infested
● There is no cure for infested plants, which should be dug up and disposed of outside the garden.

Parsnips

Carrot root fly *(see page 32)*

33

Peas

Pea moth *Cydia nigricana*
Pea moth caterpillars live and feed inside pea pods. They may damage only one or two peas, or make their way through the whole pod. They can devastate a crop grown for the production of dried peas. The moth lays its eggs in June and July on pea plants that are in flower. The tiny caterpillars quickly eat their way into developing pods, feed for a month and then return to the soil to pupate. There is only one generation a year.

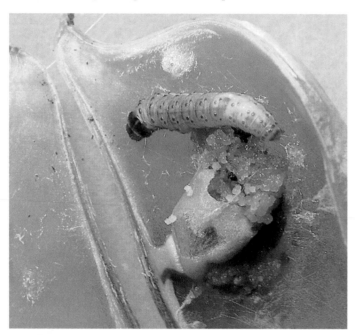

Prevention
● Sow peas early and late (eg. February and May), so they are not in flower in June/July.
● Winter dig infested plots.
● Cover peas with a very fine mesh netting while they are in flower especially in early July. As a last resort, see page 46.

Once infested
● There is no cure.

Pea thrips *Kakothrips robustus*
Thrips, commonly known as thunderflies, attack many crops. Those on peas and broad beans are up to 1.7 mm long and a yellow-brown colour; the larvae are yellow. They feed on leaves and pods causing the characteristic silver sheen. Pods may be distorted. Damage can be serious in hot dry weather.

Thrips overwinter in the soil. Adults emerge in late spring to lay their eggs on flower stamens. The larvae feed for two to three weeks then return

to the soil. There is one generation a year at its peak from mid-June to end-July.

Prevention
● Winter dig infested plots.
● Water plants regularly in dry spells to keep them cool and moist.
● Misting with water can help.
● Rotation; if attacks are very severe it could be worth not growing peas at all for a couple of years.

Once infested
● If the attack is very severe, see page 46.

Pea and bean weevil *Sitona lineatus*
Small 6 mm grey/brown weevils chew a scalloped edge on leaves of peas, broad beans, clovers and vetches. If plants are growing strongly they are not a problem, but a severe attack on young plants can be serious.

Weevils overwinter in plant debris, moving out in the early spring to lay eggs in the soil. The larvae feed on root nodules,' then emerge as adults in June and July. There is one generation a year.

Prevention
● Encourage strong fast growth.

Once infested
● As a last resort, see page 46.

Potatoes

Cyst eelworm (potato sickness) *Globodera spp.*
This microscopic pest feeds on potato roots, stunting growth and reducing crops. Effects can be severe. If you examine the roots at the end of June/ early July you may see small brown or white pinhead cysts. These fall back into the soil where they can survive for at least ten years.

Prevention
● Buy only certified seed tubers.

Once infested
● It is impossible to eliminate eelworm from the soil, but there are various strategies that can help produce some form of crop in infested soil:
● Use as long a rotation as possible.
● Grow early varieties, which do most of their growing before the eelworm attacks.
● Increase levels of organic matter in soil.
● Use the no-dig method of growing under a straw/hay mulch.
● Resistant varieties are of limited use as they are only resistant to one type of cyst eelworm.

Fruit pests, crop by crop

This chapter should be used with the identification charts at the back of this book, see pages 40-43.

Blackberries, raspberries and hybrid berries

Raspberry beetle *Byturus tomentosus*
Adults are found feeding on blossoms in May but it is the larvae that do the most damage. These tunnel into ripening fruit, occasionally causing distortion, but often not noticed until the fruit is picked. Larvae are small (up to 8 mm) and dun-coloured with brown heads and brown side markings. They overwinter in soil near canes.

Actual size x 6

Prevention
● If larvae are noticed during picking, lightly cultivate soil near canes during autumn/winter to expose pupae to birds.

Once infested
● Spray as a last resort, *(see page 46).*

Cane midge *Resseliella theobaldi*
Tiny orange/red larvae no more than 4 mm long feed in cracks in the bark of new canes. Immediate damage is light but cane blight often invades damaged areas causing canes to die back. Adults emerge from soil in May or June and lay eggs in wounds and crevices on canes. Larvae feed for a month before pupating in soil. This cycle may be repeated three times or more between July and the end of summer.

Prevention
● Lightly cultivate soil around base of canes during winter to expose pupae to birds.

Once infested
● Only spray as a last resort, *(see page 46).*

Froghoppers *Philaenus spumarius*
Most gardeners will be familiar with the white frothy blobs of 'cuckoo spit' that appear first in May. Inside each of these blobs is a nymph of the froghopper, aptly named for its shape and habit of jumping when disturbed. Generally cuckoo spit is found on ornamental plants, but raspberries and blackberries are frequently affected. The damage to the plant is minimal, despite the alarming appearance of numerous white blobs. If you are keen to get rid of them, a flick of the finger or jet of water will dislodge them.

Blackcurrants

Gall mite (big bud) *Cecidophyopsis ribis*
Mites breed inside developing buds causing them to become characteristically round and swollen, hence the term 'big bud'. Mites carry reversion virus, which is altogether more serious and will cause slow deterioration of the bush and poor cropping.

The mites overwinter in swollen buds, dispersing as these open in March and April to enter young developing buds between then and the end of June. They are sometimes carried in on the wind, by aphids and on birds' feet.

Prevention
● For new plantings buy in good quality bushes from a reputable source.

- Never plant new bushes near infested stock.
- Prevention is impossible on established bushes.

Once infested
- Remove and burn all swollen buds before spring. In severe cases cut back all growth to ground level and burn. As blackcurrants fruit on last year's wood, this will, of course, mean no crop in the following season, but the sacrifice is justified if the pest is controlled.

Leaf midge *Dasineura tetensi*
Tiny orange or white larvae infest top-most leaves on terminal shoots causing leaves to twist, distort and become speckled. Terminal shoots occasionally die and growth can be reduced.

Midges emerge from cocoons in the soil early in spring and lay eggs on unopened leaves at tips of shoots. Larvae hatch a week later, feed for a month and drop to the soil to pupate. This cycle is repeated three or four times until August or September.

Prevention
- Variety Ben Sarek has some resistance. Other resistant varieties are being developed.
- Encourage anthocorid bugs which prey on midges.

Once infested
- Spray as a last resort, *(see page 46)*.

Gooseberries

Gooseberry sawfly *Nematus ribesii*
Sawfly larvae can strip leaves on gooseberries and currants very efficiently if unchecked. The larvae are pale green with black spots and reach a final size of about 2.5 cm. Adult flies hatch from cocoons in the soil in April and lay white eggs on backs of leaves along veins, mainly low in the centre of the bush. Hatching larvae feed and create easily

spotted pin-hole effects on leaves. Mature larvae pupate in the soil. There may be three or four generations each year from late April to early September.

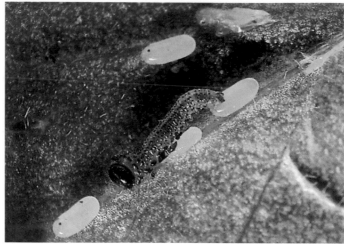

Actual size x 2

Prevention
- None.

Once infested
- Inspect bushes regularly at end of April, early June, late June/early July and early September. Pick off pin-holed leaves and crush eggs.
- Spray as a last resort, *(see page 46)*.

Magpie moth *Abraxas grossulariata*
Similar damage to gooseberry sawfly, April to June.

Caterpillars are black, white and yellow 'loopers'.

See 'sawfly' on this page for details of how to deal with this pest.

Strawberries

Red spider mite *Tetranychus urticae*
Normally a pest in greenhouses, this mite can be troublesome on outdoor strawberries (also raspberries and currants) in a hot year. The under-surfaces of the leaves are discoloured and bronzed

Actual size x 7

and older leaves become brown and withered, or crisp. A magnifying glass will reveal the tiny mites, which, despite their name, are greenish/transparent in colour with two distinct spots. Only the overwintering females are bright orange/red. They breed on leaves during the spring and summer, hibernating in crevices over winter.

Prevention
● Cut off all leaves after fruit is harvested.
● Clear up thoroughly in autumn, removing any mulch and old leaves.

Once infested
● Phytoseiulus persimilis, the predatory mite normally used to control mites in the greenhouse, can be used outside in a good summer if introduced in late June or July.

Apples

Codling moth *Cydia pomonella*
A widespread pest, principally of apples, but also affecting pears and quinces. The traditional maggot in the apple. Adults hatch from cocoons in crevices and cracks in June/July to lay eggs on leaves and fruit. Caterpillars tunnel into maturing fruit and feed there for several weeks before pupating, making fruit unsuitable for storing and particularly unappetising. In a hot summer a second generation will hatch in August.

Prevention
● Pheromone traps, which are available to the gardener, will catch many male moths and thus reduce the egg-laying potential of females, see picture on page 19. The traps are hung in a tree from mid-May until the end of July, or early September in a hot dry year.

Once infested
● Traps are insufficient for large populations of moths, or large numbers of trees, but give a good indication of when to spray for best effect. Only spray as a last resort *(see page 46)*.

Fruit tree red spider mite *Panonychus ulmi*
These mites affect apples, pears, plums and damsons causing initial speckling and bronzing of leaves and finally drying of leaves which fall prematurely. Mites overwinter as eggs, sometimes visible as small red clusters, and hatch out during April to June. The worst effects are normally seen in June and July but continue until September when the fourth or fifth generation lay eggs to overwinter.

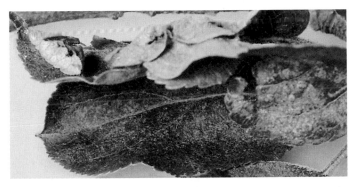

The folded leaves at the top of the picture show tortrix moth damage. The leaves below are infested with spider mite.

Prevention
● Encourage beneficial predators such as Typhlodromid mites and Anthocorid bugs which effectively keep pest numbers down. Avoid frequent use of Derris.

Once infested
● Difficult. Inspect leaves with magnifying glass in May/June. If only a few leaves are affected, pick off and destroy. Use a spray as a last resort *(see page 46)*.

Apple sawfly *Hoplocampa testudinea*
Similar damage to the codling moth, but earlier in the season. The cavities in the fruit are filled with 'frass'. Most affected fruitlets drop early, helping the thinning process, but some remain to develop into mature fruit with characteristic ribbon scarring and distortions.

Cocoons in the soil hatch in spring and the adult flies lay eggs in open blossoms in April/May. Eggs hatch two weeks later at about petal fall and the larvae tunnel immediately into fruitlets, feeding on flesh and seeds. Each larvae may visit several fruitlets before dropping to the soil in June or July to form cocoons.

Prevention
● Pick up and compost all fallen fruitlets in June and July.

Once infested
● Use a spray as a last resort, (*see page 46*).

Winter moths
Operophtera brumata, Alsophila aescularia, Erannis defoliaria

Three different moth species are responsible for similar damage to apples, pears, plums and several ornamental plants. In spring buds, blossom and young leaves are eaten by looper caterpillars coloured green, yellow or brown. Leaves become distorted and tattered and blossom fails. If disturbed, caterpillars often drop on a thread to avoid detection. Females are wingless and emerge from the soil between October and April, depending on the species, and climb the trunk or tree stake to lay eggs near buds or in cracks in the bark. March moth eggs are laid on twigs in visible bracelets. Larvae hatch in spring and feed until about June when they drop to the soil on threads to pupate.

Prevention
● Grease bands on trunks and tree stakes will catch female moths climbing up the trunk. Have them in place by late October and keep them tacky until the end of April.

Once infested
● Pick off caterpillars by hand.
● Use a spray as a last resort, (*see page 46*).

38

Tortrix moth
Archips podana, Adoxophyes orana, Pammene rhediefla

Another group of moths of distinct species causing similar damage to apples, pears, plums and cherries. It is often not serious. Green caterpillars up to 2.5 cm long feed on buds and leaves and tunnel into fruit during the summer. Leaves are drawn together with threads to protect the feeding site. Female moths lay eggs on leaves in the summer and caterpillars from these feed for a month before pupating. The next generation emerges in autumn and caterpillars born from this generation survive the winter in cocoons and feed on buds and young leaves in the spring.

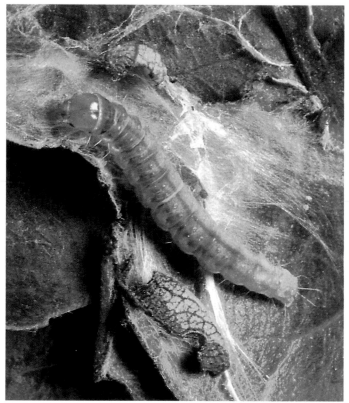

Actual size x 5

Prevention
● None.

Once infested
● Pick off caterpillars, investigating "webbed" leaves carefully. Webbing of leaves makes spraying impractical. Damage is usually not serious.

Cherries

Pear and cherry slugworm
(*see 'Pears' on page 39*).

Pears

Codling moth *(see 'Apples' on page 37)*

Fruit tree red spider mite
(see 'Apples' on page 37).

Leaf blister mites *Eriophyes pyri*
Pink or yellow/green pustules show on leaves in May, turning dark and causing leaf fall later. Tiny mites are feeding within the leaves to cause these blisters.

Adults overwinter in buds and start feeding on leaves in spring. Developing colonies continue to feed through the summer.

Prevention
● None.

Once infested
● Pick off affected leaves early. No other cure available. Damage seldom serious.

Pear midge *Contarinia pyrivora*
Orange-white larvae of this midge feed within the fruitlets causing them to swell, blacken and drop. It can be a serious pest in southern England .

Cocoons in soil over winter give rise to adults in March/April. Females fly into trees and lay eggs in unopened flower buds. The larvae hatch out within the developing fruitlet, for a month or so. After about six weeks they tunnel their way out of the fruitlet, which may already have dropped to the ground. They move into the soil to form cocoons, where they spend the winter.

Prevention
● Pick up and compost all fallen fruitlets during the summer.
● Remove affected fruitlets immediately they are noticed.
● Cultivate soil near affected trees in winter to expose cocoons.

Once infested
● There is no cure.

Pear and cherry slugworm *Caliroa cerasi*
During late spring and summer, the upper surfaces of pear and cherry leaves are grazed to a skeleton by small shiny black larvae resembling slugs which later turn waxy yellow.

Adult flies emerge from cocoons in the soil between May and June and lay eggs on the leaves. Larvae from these feed for a month and then pupate in the soil. The second generation emerges in July/August.

Actual size x 5

Prevention
● If pests have been seen, cultivate soil lightly near affected trees.

Once infested
● Pick off pests,
● Use a spray as a last resort, (see page 46).

Winter moth and Tortrix moth
(see 'Apples' on page 38).

Plums and damsons

Fruit moth *Cydia funebrana*
These are similar in life cycle and type of damage to Codling moth *(see page 37)*. Pinky red maggots feed inside plums and damsons in July/August causing early ripening and falling of fruit.

Prevention
● Pick up and compost all early falling fruit whilst caterpillars are still present.

Once infested
● There is no cure.

Fruit tree red spider mite
(see 'Apples' on page 37).

Plum sawfly *Hoplocampa flava*
A cousin of the apple sawfly. Similar damage to the plum fruit moth in spring and early summer, leaving sticky exudate from the entry hole in later stages.

Life cycle is similar to apple sawfly.

Prevention
● Pick up all early fallen fruit as for fruit moth. Damage varies from year to year.

Once infested
● Use a spray as a last resort, as for apple sawfly *(see page 46)*.

Tortrix moth and Winter moth
(see 'Apples' on page 38).

Identifying vegetable pests at a glance

NAME	SYMPTOM	CAUSE	PAGE
Seedlings, general It is often difficult to know why seedlings fail to emerge, or die once they have done so. Maybe the initial seed was poor, or growing conditions were unsuitable; or they may have been attacked by a number of non-specific pests and diseases. When a problem cannot be identified, the best line of defence is to help them to get a good start, (*see page 14*).	Seedlings fail to appear. Seedlings grow poorly or collapse and die. Stems and/or roots chewed. Seedlings with leaves and growing points eaten, Seedlings, especially brassicas, peas and beans, pecked and pulled out of soil.	Mice Birds Bean seed fly Millipedes Cutworm Wireworm Millipedes Slugs Birds	23 21 28 24 22 27 24 25 21
Asparagus	Leaves and stems eaten. Chequered beetles and/or grey/black larvae may be seen.	Asparagus beetle	28
Beans (French, broad and runner) and peas (*see also 'Seedings'*)	Semicircular notches eaten out of leaf margins (peas, broad beans). Shoots and leaves infested with small black insects; may be sticky. Leaves and pods with light flecking or silvery sheen (peas, broad beans). Flowers full of small shiny black beetles. Pods with triangular pieces pecked away. Pea pods with small, black-headed caterpillars inside; peas eaten.	Pea and bean weevil Blackfly Thrips Blossom beetles Birds Pea moth	34 28 34 29 21 34
Beetroot and spinach beet (*see also 'Seedings'*)	Leaves and stems infested with small black insects. Blotchy brown blisters on leaves. Roots have irregular holes.	Black bean aphid Beet leaf miner Cutworm Swiftmoth	29 29 22 26
Brassicas (*see also 'Seedings'*)	Leaves of seedlings and young plants show pitting and small circular holes. Leaves torn, often reduced to a skeleton of veins. Transplants may be pulled out. Leaves with irregular holes eaten out. Leaves with irregular holes and slime trails. Leaves infested with colonies of floury grey insects; may be discoloured and distorted. Seedlings and young plants grow poorly and may wilt. Easily pulled up to show roots absent, or being eaten by white maggots. Leaves, especially underside, infested with small white insects which fly up when disturbed. Calabrese heads grazed by hordes of tiny black beetles.	Flea beetle Birds Caterpillars Slugs Mealy cabbage aphid Cabbage root fly Whitefly Blossom beetles	31 21 30 25 29 30 31 29

40

Carrots and parsnips (*see also 'Seedings'*) The following symptoms can be found on both carrots and parsnips, unless stated.	Carrot leaves with red/yellow mottling; may be twisted; plants stunted.	Carrot root fly	32
	Carrot leaves infested with small green insects.	Carrot willow aphid	20
	Irregular holes in roots; caterpillars in nearby soil.	Cutworm	22
		Swift moth caterpillar	26
	Roots tunnelled by small white maggots.	Carrot root fly	32
Celery and celeriac (*see also 'Seedings'*)	Plants collapse; stems eaten off at ground level.	Cutworm	22
	Stems chewed; slime trails visible.	Slugs	25
	Leaves show yellowy-brown blotchy 'mines' which may contain small larvae	Celery leaf miner	32
	Plants collapse, roots and stem base tunnelled by small maggots.	Carrot root fly	32
Lettuce (*see also 'Seedings'*)	Seedlings and larger plants unthrifty.	Wireworm	27
		Millipedes	24
	Plants wilt and die; stem eaten off at ground level.	Cutworm	22
	Plants wilt and die; stem eaten.	Swift moth caterpillar	26
	Leaves infested with small pink or green insects.	Aphids	33
	Plants stunted; may wilt suddenly.	Root aphids	33
Onions, leeks, chives, garlic and shallots, etc.	Seedlings and leaves attacked at or below ground level.	Wireworm	27
		Cutworm	22
	Leaves wilt, small white maggots in base of bulb.	Onion fly	33
	Base of plant swells early; leaves swollen and distorted.	Stem eelworm	33
Parsley	Leaves with reddish tinge, growth poor; roots tunnelled by small white maggots.	Carrot root fly	32
	Leaves with brown blotchy 'blisters' which may contain larvae.	Celery fly	32
Parsnip (*see also 'Carrots and parsnips'*)	Leaves with yellow-brown blotchy 'mines' which may contain small white larvae.	Celery leaf miner	32
Peas (*see 'Beans and peas'*)			
Potatoes	Leaves yellow, growth poor, crops reduced.	Potato cyst eelworm	34
		Pin-head cysts may be seen on roots.	
	Tubers with holes and galleries which may extend throughout.	Slugs	25
	Tubers with large holes near surface.	Cutworm	22
		Swift moth caterpillar	26
	Tubers gnawed; tooth marks may be visible.	Mice	23
	Tubers with narrow holes, as if made by a knitting needle.	Wireworm	27
Spinach, annual (*see also 'Seedings'*)	Leaves with blotchy brown 'blisters' which may have larvae inside.	Leaf miner	29

NAME	SYMPTOM	CAUSE	PAGE
Apples	Leaves and shoots infested with small green or pink insects; leaves feel sticky and may be distorted.	Aphids	20
	Leaves and petals chewed; fruit with small 'glassy' patches, punctured with tiny black holes.	Earwigs	22
	Leaves speckled, bronzed or dried up; tiny mites on undersides.	Fruit tree red spider mite	37
	Leaves/shoots with blobs of white froth.	Froghoppers	35
	Young leaves with irregular tattered holes; fruits partly distorted or with raised bumps and discoloured patches.	Capsid bugs	21
	Young leaves tattered in spring; shiny beetles present.	Leaf weevils	27
	Young leaves, flowers and buds eaten; 'loopers' present.	Winter moth	38
	Leaves bound together tightly by threads; caterpillar inside.	Tortrix moth	38
	Fruitlets holed, wet frass in hole, fall prematurely; fruits with ribbon scarring.	Apple sawfly	37
	Fruit with core rotten and tunnelled. Maggot may be present inside.	Codling moth	37
	Fruits with large holes or small pieces chewed or removed.	Birds Wasps	21 26
	Tunnelling under tree; roots damaged.	Voles	23
Blackberries, raspberries and hybrid berries	Underside of leaves infested with small pale green insects; leaves sticky.	Aphids	20
	Dun-coloured larvae feeding in fruits.	Raspberry beetle	35
	Tiny orange/red larvae feeding in cracks in bark of new raspberry canes; tunnelling found in old canes when pruned out.	Cane midge	35
	Leaves with irregular holes	Capsid bugs	21
	Ripe fruits chewed.	Wasps	26
	Leaves/shoots with blobs of white froth.	Froghoppers	35
	Young leaves on fruiting canes chewed by tiny weevils in spring.	Leaf weevils	27
	Leaves speckled, bronzed or dried up; tiny mites on undersides.	Spider mites	37
Blackcurrants	Shoot tips infested with green or yellow insects; leaves curled over and sticky, possibly blistered or distorted.	Aphids	20
	Youngest leaves curled over tightly, speckled and failing to develop.	Leaf midge	36
	Buds swollen and round in winter.	Gall mite	35
	Fruit removed.	Birds	21
	Leaves with irregular holes, especially young leaves.	Capsid bugs	21
Cherries	Tips of shoots infested with black insects; leaves curled over and sticky.	Aphids	20
	Surface of leaves grazed by small, black slug-like larvae.	Pear and cherry slugworm	39
	Buds pecked out in winter; few flowers and lengths of bare branch in spring.	Bullfinches	21

Gooseberries, redcurrants and whitecurrants	Leaves stripped and skeletonized, large numbers of caterpillars present.	Gooseberry sawfly Magpie moth	36 36
	Leaves with irregular holes, especially young leaves.	Capsid bugs	21
	Shoot tips infested with tiny insects; leaves sticky, curled, distorted, sometimes blackened.	Aphids	20
	Buds pecked out in winter; poor blossom and bare lengths of branch in spring.	Bullfinches	21
	Tunnelling under tree; roots damaged.	Voles	23
Pears	Leaves and shoots infested with small grey, black or brown insects; leaves feel sticky and may be distorted.	Aphids	20
	Leaves speckled, bronzed or dried up; tiny insects on undersides.	Fruit tree red spider mite	37
	Young leaves in spring tattered and chewed; shiny beetles present.	Leaf weevils	27
	Leaves/shoots with blobs of white froth.	Froghoppers	35
	Young leaves, flowers and buds eaten; 'loopers' present.	Winter moth	38
	Leaves bound together tightly by threads; caterpillar inside.	Tortrix moth	38
	Leaf surfaces grazed by small, black, slug-like larvae.	Pear and cherry	
	Leaves with yellow/brown blisters.	Leaf blister mite	39
	Fruitlets swollen and distorted, fall prematurely; small maggots inside.	Pear midge	39
	Fruits tunnelled; maggot inside.	Codling moth	37
	Fruits with irregular bumps and scars.	Capsid bugs	21
	Fruits pecked or chewed.	Birds Wasps	21 26
	Tunnelling under tree; roots damaged.	Voles	23
Plums and damsons	Leaves and shoots infested with green or green and yellow insects and sticky; leaves very tightly curled and distorted.	Aphids	20
	Leaves speckled, bronzed or dried up; tiny insects on undersides.	Fruit tree red spider mite	37
	Young leaves tattered in spring; shiny beetles present.	Leaf weevils	27
	Leaves with small ragged holes especially at shoot tips; fruits misshapen.	Capsid bugs	21
	Young leaves, flowers and buds eaten; 'loopers' present.	Winter moth	38
	Leaves bound together by threads.	Tortrix moth	38
	Fruitlets tunnelled, wet frass near entrance; fruitlets fall early.	Plum sawfly	39
	Fruits tunnelled; maggot inside.	Plum fruit moth	39
	Fruits pecked or chewed.	Birds Wasps	21 26
	Buds removed in winter; poor blossom and bare lengths of branch in winter.	Bullfinches	21
	Tunnelling under tree; roots damaged.	Voles	23
Strawberries	Underside of leaves covered in tiny pale-coloured insects; leaves sticky and possibly sooty.	Aphids	20
	Fruits partially or wholly eaten away.	Birds Wasps Snails and slugs	21 26 25
	Plants wilting; white or pale yellow larvae feeding on roots.	Wireworm	27
	Leaves yellowing and bronzing; minute mites on undersides.	Red spider mite	37

Organic pesticides

Safer sprays?

The sprays included here can be used in commercial organic production, according to the standards set by the Soil Association (SA) and the United Kingdom Register of Organic Food Standards (UKROFS). The Soil Association standards do, however, put them in a 'restricted' category, not for routine use. This is because they are not harmless. They may be less harmful and less persistent than many, but they are poisons and will, inevitably, harm creatures other than those we wish to kill. 'Organic' pesticides should be used with restraint, and should not be seen as an alternative to the many other organic methods that have been introduced in this book.

Effective spraying

All pesticides, whatever their nature, should be used correctly. This is essential both to ensure that they are effective, and also so that harm to the environment is minimized.

● Do's

Identify the problem first, then choose an appropriate spray.

Read the label and instructions carefully before opening the bottle.

Use a sprayer suitable for the job – one that is in good condition, gives a good even spray and does not leak.

Use the exact dilutions recommended and only make up the quantity of spray that you need.

Adjust the sprayer so that it gives good cover of the area being sprayed. Too coarse a spray will mean that a lot of the spray just runs off the plant; too fine a spray may result in the spray drifting on to other plants.

Spray in still weather to reduce spray drift.

Apply the spray to the relevant area. If a spray only works by direct contact with a pest there is no point in spraying parts of the plant that are not infested.

Store pesticides in their original packaging, in a secure, cool, dark place.

● Don'ts

Use a spray just because it is the only one you have at the time.

Use a spray against pests other than those for which it is recommended.

Add a little bit extra 'just in case' when diluting a pesticide.

Store made up pesticides.

Spray in windy weather.

Spray plants where bees are working.

Store pesticides in unmarked bottles and in places accessible to children.

Pesticides and bees
Pesticides are harmful to bees. To avoid killing or injuring these useful creatures, *never spray a crop where bees are working*. This means that when plants are in flower they should not be sprayed. If it is essential to spray, only do so in the evening when the bees have finished working. Alternatively spray on cool early mornings when the bees are less active.

If there are bee keepers in your neighbourhood, give them advance warning of any spraying.